EXPLAIN LIKE I'M 5

BLOCKCHAINS & CRYPTOCURRENCIES

Eric Tennever

Introduction

Hey there! So you've probably heard a lot of buzzwords floating around like "Bitcoin," "blockchain," or even "cryptocurrency." It can feel like everyone's talking about it, but no one's explaining what it actually is—in a way that's easy to understand.

That's what this book is for. We're going to break things down into bite-sized pieces and make sense of this whole blockchain and cryptocurrency thing. Whether you're just curious or thinking about dipping your toes into the world of crypto, you're in the right place.

Let's get something clear from the start: blockchain and cryptocurrency are not the same thing. A blockchain is a technology—a system that can do lots of cool things beyond powering cryptocurrencies like Bitcoin. On the other hand, cryptocurrencies are just one of the most famous uses of blockchains, but there's so much more to explore.

Think of blockchains like the internet itself. You can use the internet for emails, shopping, or even watching cat videos. Similarly, blockchains can be used for all kinds of things, and cryptocurrencies are just one "app" in the blockchain world.

Over the next few chapters, I'll walk you through what blockchains are, why they're such a big deal, how cryptocurrencies fit in, and what the future might look like with these technologies. I promise, you won't need a computer science degree to understand any of it! We'll keep things light, simple, and maybe even a little fun.

So buckle up—by the end of this book, you'll not only know what all the fuss is about, but you'll also have a good sense of how blockchain and cryptocurrencies could change the world.

Chapter 1: What Even Is a Blockchain?

Ever heard someone explain something in a way that made you more confused than before? Yeah, blockchain can feel like that at first. But trust me, it's not that complicated. Let's start from scratch.

Ever had someone explain something so confusing that you're left scratching your head even more? Yeah, that happens a lot with blockchain—but it doesn't have to. It might seem like some complicated tech magic, but once we break it down, it's really not that hard to grasp. Let's start from square one.

WHAT IS A BLOCK?

Okay, picture this: you have a digital notebook, and every time something important happens—a payment, a contract agreement, or even a document transfer—you write it down. Every single note you jot down is a "block." It's essentially a piece of data recording something that took place.

For example, let's say Alice sends Bob $50. That transaction gets written down as a block. Simple, right? A block is just a small record of something that happened digitally.

WHAT IS A CHAIN?

Now here's where it gets a little more interesting. Instead of all these blocks floating around on their own, they get linked together in order, creating a "chain." Think of it like your digital notebook having a table of contents that records the exact sequence of every event.

Once a block is written down, it's locked in place. You can't just go back and edit it or rearrange things without messing up the entire chain.

Imagine you're writing in ink, not pencil—once something is recorded, it's permanent. This "chain" is what makes blockchain so trustworthy. It's like a diary that keeps everything in perfect order and doesn't let you scribble anything out later.

THE UNBREAKABLE LINK

Now, to make things even more secure, each block gets its own special code—a unique fingerprint called a "hash." But there's more: each block also carries the fingerprint of the previous block. This clever linking process is what creates the chain.

So, if someone tries to change one block (say, Bob tries to pretend Alice didn't send him that

$50), they'd have to change every single block before it. That's nearly impossible, especially since all the computers (or nodes) in the network have copies of the entire blockchain. Everyone in the network would immediately know something fishy was going on, and they'd reject the tampered block. This is why blockchains are considered *super* secure—it's like trying to rewrite history without anyone noticing. Good luck with that!

Chapter 2: Why Blockchains Are Such a Big Deal (Even Beyond Crypto!)

Alright, now you might be thinking, "Okay, I get what a blockchain is, but why is it so revolutionary? Why does everyone keep saying it's going to change everything?" Good questions! Let's dig into why blockchains are so special.

BLOCKCHAINS WORK WITHOUT A MIDDLEMAN

Let's say you want to buy something online. Normally, you'd need to trust a third party to handle the payment—like a bank, PayPal, or some other payment processor. These guys are the "middlemen." They take your money, verify that it's real, and then pass it along to the seller. They're basically there to make sure everyone plays fair.

But with blockchain, you don't need a middleman at all. Instead of relying on a bank to verify your transaction, the blockchain network takes care of it. The transaction is recorded as a block, and the network—made up of many computers—checks and verifies it. This process is called decentralization, and it's one of the coolest things about blockchain. No single company or person controls the system. Everyone on the network keeps each other in check.

By cutting out the middleman, transactions become faster, cheaper, and often more secure. Plus, it gives people more control over their own money or data, instead of handing control to a central authority.

IT'S NOT JUST ABOUT MONEY

So, blockchain can handle payments without needing a bank—that's great. But it doesn't stop there. One of the most exciting things about blockchain is that it can be used for *so much more* than just moving money around.

Let's take voting, for example. Elections are super important, and yet, they're vulnerable to fraud or manipulation. But with a blockchain, every vote could be a block, securely recorded in a way that can't be tampered with. Each vote would be verified by the network, and once recorded, no one could change it. You'd have a transparent, trustworthy election process where everyone can verify the results.

Or how about supply chains? When you buy a product, wouldn't it be great to know exactly where it came from? With blockchain, you can. Let's say you're buying a new pair of shoes. Every step of the production process—from the factory to the shipping company, to the store—could be recorded on a blockchain. You could scan a code and see the entire journey your shoes took, making it easier to check if the product is ethically sourced or if it's a fake. It's transparency on a whole new level.

REAL-WORLD USE CASES

Blockchain is already being used in some pretty fascinating ways. Some companies use it to verify diamonds, ensuring they aren't sourced from conflict zones. Others are using blockchain to secure medical records, making sure only the right people can access sensitive health information. Even climate change fighters are getting in on the action, using blockchain to track carbon emissions and verify green projects.

We're still in the early stages, but the potential of blockchain technology is huge. It's not just about cryptocurrencies anymore—it's a tool that could reshape industries, enhance transparency, and build more trust in systems that we rely on every day.

So, when people talk about blockchain being a game-changer, they're not just talking about Bitcoin. They're talking about a technology that could power the future of how we buy, sell, vote, work, and live.

Chapter 3: How Does Blockchain Keep Data Safe?

So far, we've covered what a blockchain is and why it's such a big deal. But one thing you might still be wondering is, "How can people trust a blockchain if no single person or company is in charge?" That's a great question—and the answer is one of the coolest things about blockchain: it lets you trust the system without needing to trust any one person or organization.

This chapter is all about the magic of how blockchain stays secure and trustworthy without relying on a central authority, like a bank or government.

DECENTRALIZATION: EVERYONE'S WATCHING

Let's start with the idea of decentralization. In a traditional system—like your bank—the bank acts as the authority. They have the master ledger that tracks all the transactions, and we trust them to keep it accurate and secure.

But in a blockchain system, instead of having one central ledger (or record of transactions), everyone in the network has a copy of the blockchain. These participants are often called "nodes." Each node is like its own mini bank, keeping track of every transaction that happens in the system. This means no single person or company holds all the power, and that makes it much harder for anyone to manipulate the system.

Think of it like this: Imagine you're playing a game of Monopoly with friends. Instead of one person being in charge of keeping track of everyone's money, **everyone** writes down every transaction on their own notepad. If one person tries to cheat and says they have more money than they actually do, everyone else will look at their notes and call them out. That's how decentralization works in blockchain—everyone is keeping an eye on everyone else, so no one can pull a fast one.

CONSENSUS MECHANISMS: HOW THE NETWORK AGREES

But wait—how do all these computers (or nodes) agree on which transactions are valid and which ones aren't? After all, there's no central referee to make the call. This is where consensus mechanisms come in.

There are different types of consensus mechanisms, but the two most common are:

Proof-of-Work (PoW)

Proof-of-Work is like a high-stakes puzzle-solving contest. When a new block of transactions is ready to be added to the blockchain, all the computers in the network compete to solve a really difficult math problem. It's so tough that it requires a lot of computing power to solve.

The first computer to solve the problem gets to add the block to the blockchain and is rewarded with cryptocurrency (like Bitcoin). This process is called mining (we'll dive more into that in a later chapter). Once the block is added, all the other computers check the solution to make sure it's correct. If it is, they all agree that the block should be added to the blockchain, and the process starts over with the next block.

Why does this make the system secure? Because solving these puzzles takes a lot of work (hence the name Proof-of-Work). If a hacker wanted to mess with the blockchain, they'd have to solve the puzzle for not just one block, but every block in the chain—an almost impossible task because it would require an enormous amount of computing power and energy.

Proof-of-Stake (PoS)

Proof-of-Stake is a more eco-friendly alternative to Proof-of-Work. Instead of computers racing to solve puzzles, people who own some cryptocurrency can "stake" it, like putting down a deposit. The system then randomly picks one of these stakers to verify the next block of transactions.

If they do the job correctly, they get rewarded with more cryptocurrency. If they try to cheat, they lose some of their staked coins. It's a bit like putting up collateral—you're motivated to play fair because if you don't, you'll lose something valuable. This system is more energy-efficient because it doesn't require massive amounts of computing power to run.

Both Proof-of-Work and Proof-of-Stake are ways to ensure that the network reaches agreement (or **consensus**) on which transactions are valid and which aren't—without needing a central authority to oversee things.

IMMUTABILITY: WHY BLOCKCHAINS CAN'T BE TAMPERED WITH

Now, let's talk about one of the most powerful features of a blockchain: immutability. In simple terms, immutability means that once a block is added to the blockchain, it can't be changed. It's locked in place forever, like carving something in stone.

Here's how it works: Every block has a unique code, called a hash, which acts like its digital fingerprint. It also contains the hash of the previous block. This is what creates the chain-like structure we talked about earlier.

If someone tried to go back and change a transaction in a block (like altering the amount of money sent or changing who received it), it would change that block's hash. And since each block's hash is linked to the one before it, changing one block would mess up the entire chain. The system would immediately recognize that something's wrong, and the change would be rejected.

This is what makes blockchain so secure—it's extremely difficult to go back and tamper with past transactions. To successfully change a block, you'd have to change all the blocks that came after it as well, which would require an almost unimaginable amount of computing power. In a decentralized system with thousands of nodes, this is nearly impossible.

THE TRUST WITHOUT TRUST SYSTEM

One of the most mind-blowing things about blockchain is that it creates trust without needing to trust. Sounds confusing, right? Here's what it means: In traditional systems, like banks, we trust them because they're regulated, they have a reputation, and they have systems in place to correct mistakes. We trust that they'll handle our money responsibly.

With blockchain, you don't have to trust any single person or company. The technology itself is what you trust. The blockchain's decentralization, consensus mechanisms, and immutability make it incredibly secure, without needing to trust a middleman. The system ensures that once a transaction is verified and added to the blockchain, it's almost impossible to alter or erase.

WHY THIS MATTERS

This ability to trust a system without relying on a single authority has huge implications. It means we can create financial systems, voting systems, or even supply chains where no one has the power to manipulate or tamper with the data. It also opens up possibilities for people who might not trust traditional institutions, like those in countries with corrupt governments or unstable currencies.

Blockchain has redefined the concept of trust in a digital world. It's no longer about trusting a central authority—it's about trusting the network, the math, and the technology itself. And that's a pretty revolutionary idea.

Chapter 4: How Cryptocurrencies Were Born (Blockchain's First Major Use)

Now that you understand what a blockchain is, let's talk about the first big thing people used it for: cryptocurrency. And it all starts with the legendary story of Bitcoin.

A DIGITAL CASH PROBLEM

Before Bitcoin, people had been trying to figure out digital money for years. The big problem with digital cash is trust. How do you make sure someone doesn't spend the same digital dollar twice? After all, anything digital—like a picture or a file—can be copied easily. This is called the "double-spending problem."

Normally, banks or payment systems solve this by keeping track of who spends what. But what if you didn't want to rely on a bank? How do you create digital money that doesn't need a central authority to keep things straight?

ENTER SATOSHI NAKAMOTO

In 2008, someone (or some group of people) going by the name Satoshi Nakamoto published a paper that outlined a way to solve the double-spending problem without needing a bank or middleman. This was the birth of Bitcoin.

Satoshi's idea was simple but brilliant: use a blockchain to record every single Bitcoin transaction. Because the blockchain is decentralized, no single person or company controls it. This means you don't need a bank to verify transactions—the network does it for you!

THE FIRST CRYPTOCURRENCY: BITCOIN

Bitcoin became the first cryptocurrency, which is just a fancy word for digital money that uses encryption (secure codes) to control how it's created and spent. Bitcoin transactions are recorded on a public blockchain, which means everyone can see what's happening, but no one can mess with the records. And because the system relies on the blockchain's security, people trust it to work without a bank.

WHY BITCOIN MATTERED

The introduction of Bitcoin was revolutionary. It wasn't just about making digital payments possible—it was about creating a whole new kind of money that wasn't controlled by any government or bank. For some, this represented freedom from the traditional financial system, and that's part of why it gained so much attention.

Plus, Bitcoin's supply is limited. There will only ever be 21 million Bitcoins, making it kind of like digital gold. This scarcity is one reason people see Bitcoin as valuable.

THE FIRST TRANSACTION: PIZZA!

Fun fact: the first real-world Bitcoin purchase was for two pizzas in 2010. Someone paid 10,000 Bitcoins (worth millions today!) for two pizzas. It shows how far we've come from Bitcoin being a niche experiment to a widely recognized digital currency.

Chapter 5:

Bitcoin: The King of Cryptos

Let's take a closer look at Bitcoin, the cryptocurrency that started it all. Today, Bitcoin is often called "digital gold" because, like gold, people view it as a store of value. But how does Bitcoin actually work, and why do so many people trust it?

HOW BITCOIN WORKS ON THE BLOCKCHAIN

Every time you send or receive Bitcoin, you're creating a new block in Bitcoin's blockchain. Think of it like writing a new line in a shared ledger. This ledger is public, meaning anyone can see it, but it's also secure—only you have control over your Bitcoin.

When you want to send Bitcoin to someone, the transaction is bundled with others into a block. This block is then added to the chain of previous blocks, which contains every Bitcoin transaction ever made. It's a bit like a never-ending digital notebook where no one can erase what's been written.

WHY BITCOIN IS TRUSTED

Bitcoin is often trusted for three main reasons:

1. **Decentralization:** No single entity controls Bitcoin. Instead, it runs on a network of computers (called "nodes") all over the world. This makes it incredibly hard for any one person or group to manipulate.
2. **Limited Supply:** As mentioned earlier, there will only ever be 21 million Bitcoins. This scarcity gives it value, similar to how gold's limited supply makes it precious.

3. **Security:** Bitcoin's blockchain is nearly impossible to tamper with because of its decentralized nature and the cryptographic methods it uses to secure data. Changing a single block in the chain would require changing every block, on every computer in the network—a task so monumental, it's practically impossible.

MINING: HOW BITCOIN IS CREATED

New Bitcoins are created through a process called "mining," but this isn't like digging in the ground for gold. In the Bitcoin world, mining involves computers solving complex math problems. When a computer solves one of these problems, it gets to add a new block to the blockchain and is rewarded with newly created Bitcoins.

This process takes a lot of computing power (and energy), which is why people build entire "mining farms" with powerful computers working around the clock to mine Bitcoin.

BITCOIN AS DIGITAL GOLD

Many people don't see Bitcoin as just a way to buy stuff. They see it as a store of value—something you hold onto because you believe its value will increase over time. That's why Bitcoin is often compared to gold. Just like gold, Bitcoin is rare, it's valuable, and it doesn't rely on any government or central authority to maintain its value.

WHY BITCOIN CAN BE VOLATILE

Bitcoin's value can swing wildly, going up or down by thousands of dollars in a short time. This volatility can make it exciting, but also risky. One day, your Bitcoin could be worth a lot more; the next, it could drop in value. The reasons for these price swings are complicated, but they often boil down to supply and demand, speculation, and news about regulation or security.

Chapter 6: Beyond Bitcoin: The Rise of Altcoins

While Bitcoin is the most famous cryptocurrency, it's far from the only one. In fact, since Bitcoin's launch, thousands of other cryptocurrencies have been created. These are called "altcoins," which simply means "alternative coins." Some of them try to improve on Bitcoin, while others focus on completely different uses of blockchain technology.

WHAT MAKES AN ALTCOIN DIFFERENT?

Not all cryptocurrencies work the same way. While Bitcoin is focused on being a decentralized digital currency and store of value, many altcoins offer new features or improve on Bitcoin's limitations.

For example:

- **Faster Transactions:** Some altcoins are designed to process transactions more quickly than Bitcoin. Litecoin, for instance, was created to be a "lighter" version of Bitcoin with faster transaction times.
- **Cheaper Fees:** While Bitcoin can have high transaction fees during busy times, some altcoins focus on keeping fees low. Ripple (XRP), for example, aims to make international money transfers fast and cheap, especially for banks and financial institutions.
- **More Privacy:** Certain altcoins like Monero and Zcash are designed to offer enhanced privacy features. While Bitcoin's blockchain is public (meaning anyone can see transactions), these privacy coins use advanced encryption techniques to hide

details about who is sending or receiving funds.

ENTER ETHEREUM: SMART CONTRACTS AND DAPPS

Perhaps the most well-known altcoin is Ethereum. But Ethereum isn't just another form of digital money—it's a whole new kind of platform. Ethereum introduced the world to **smart contracts** and decentralized applications, or **dApps**.

- **Smart Contracts:** These are self-executing contracts with the terms of the agreement written directly into code. Imagine a vending machine: you put in money, and it automatically gives you the snack you paid for. A smart contract works similarly, but for more complex agreements—like automatically paying someone when a job is completed.

- **Decentralized Apps (dApps):** These are apps that run on a blockchain, meaning no one controls them. Once a dApp is created, it operates independently. Think of it like an app store, but without Apple or Google in charge. Developers can create dApps for anything from gaming to finance to social media, all powered by the Ethereum blockchain.

UTILITY VS. STORE OF VALUE

While Bitcoin is often called "digital gold" and seen as a store of value, many altcoins have a different purpose. Ethereum, for example, is often viewed as a platform for building things (like dApps and smart contracts), rather than just a form of money. Other altcoins might focus on things like enhancing privacy, speeding up transactions, or reducing energy usage.

This distinction between cryptocurrencies used for specific purposes (like Ethereum) and those held primarily for their value (like Bitcoin) is important when thinking about the broader cryptocurrency ecosystem.

A QUICK TOUR OF POPULAR ALTCOINS

Here are a few of the more well-known altcoins you might have heard about:

- **Litecoin (LTC):** Created as the "silver to Bitcoin's gold," Litecoin is designed to be faster and more efficient for everyday transactions.
- **Ripple (XRP):** Focused on making cross-border payments faster and cheaper, especially for banks.
- **Cardano (ADA):** A blockchain platform that uses a more eco-friendly

version of Proof-of-Stake, and focuses on academic research and security.

- **Polkadot (DOT):** Designed to allow different blockchains to work together, making it easier to transfer data and assets between different networks.
- **Solana (SOL):** Known for its extremely fast transaction speeds and low fees, making it a strong competitor for Ethereum when it comes to dApps.

Chapter 7: What Are Smart Contracts and Why Should You Care?

We've mentioned smart contracts before, but let's dive deeper into what they are and why they're such a big deal in the blockchain world. Spoiler alert: they're not actual contracts like the ones you sign with a pen—they're digital, and they can do a lot more than you might think.

WHAT IS A SMART CONTRACT?

At its core, a smart contract is a program that automatically enforces an agreement. Think of it as a set of "if-then" rules written in code. For example, "If I send you 1 Ether (Ethereum's cryptocurrency), then you send me a digital file."

Once the smart contract is created, it will execute these conditions without any need for a third party. It's self-executing, meaning the contract does all the work, no humans involved. The rules are clear and, most importantly, cannot be changed once the contract is deployed on the blockchain.

WHY SHOULD YOU CARE?

Smart contracts matter because they eliminate the need for intermediaries like banks, lawyers, or brokers. Traditionally, if you wanted to rent an apartment, for instance, you'd go through a rental agency or lawyer to make sure the contract is followed. With a smart contract, the terms are coded, and once you meet the conditions (like paying the rent), the contract automatically grants you access to the apartment without needing anyone to process it.

This has huge potential for reducing costs and speeding up transactions in many industries, from real estate to insurance to supply chain management.

HOW SMART CONTRACTS WORK IN THE REAL WORLD

Let's explore a few examples where smart contracts are already being used or could be used in the future:

- **Insurance:** Imagine you buy travel insurance. If your flight gets canceled, instead of waiting for an insurance agent to process your claim, a smart contract could automatically verify the cancellation and send your payout instantly.
- **Real Estate:** With a smart contract, buying a house could be as simple as

clicking a few buttons. Once the agreed amount of money is sent through the blockchain, the ownership of the property could automatically transfer to you without needing a lawyer or real estate agent to finalize the deal.

- **Supply Chain:** A product traveling from a factory to your door goes through many steps. A smart contract can automatically trigger payments at each step of the process, such as when the product is shipped, when it passes inspection, or when it reaches the warehouse. This ensures everything runs smoothly and transparently.

ETHEREUM: THE SMART CONTRACT PIONEER

While smart contracts can technically run on other blockchains, Ethereum is where they really took off. Ethereum is designed to be a platform for building these contracts and decentralized apps (dApps) on top of its blockchain.

Developers use Ethereum to create and deploy smart contracts that can handle everything from decentralized finance (DeFi) applications to games to digital art marketplaces (hello, NFTs!).

BENEFITS OF SMART CONTRACTS

- **Automation:** Smart contracts remove the need for middlemen. This saves time, reduces costs, and eliminates human error.
- **Transparency:** Because they run on a public blockchain, anyone can see the terms of the contract. There are no hidden clauses or surprises.
- **Security:** Once deployed, smart contracts are difficult to tamper with. The blockchain

ensures that the code runs exactly as written.

LIMITATIONS OF SMART CONTRACTS

Of course, smart contracts aren't perfect. One major issue is that they are only as good as the code they're written in. If there's a bug or error in the code, it could lead to unintended consequences. Also, once deployed, a smart contract can't be easily changed or canceled.

Smart contracts are a powerful tool, but they need to be carefully written and tested before being used in important situations.

Chapter 8: How Cryptocurrencies Are Made: Mining and Minting

By now, you might be wondering, "Where do cryptocurrencies actually come from?" Unlike traditional money, you don't just print cryptocurrencies. Instead, they are created through processes like mining or minting, depending on the type of cryptocurrency and its underlying technology.

CRYPTO MINING: DIGGING FOR DIGITAL GOLD

Let's start with Bitcoin, which is created through a process called **mining**. But we're not talking about digging through the ground with a shovel. In the crypto world, mining means solving complex math problems using computers.

Here's how it works:

- **Verification:** When people send Bitcoin to each other, their transactions get bundled together into blocks. Before these blocks can be added to the blockchain, they need to be verified. That's where miners come in. Miners use powerful computers to solve a complicated mathematical puzzle that verifies the transactions in the block.
- **Competition:** It's a race! The first miner to solve the puzzle gets to add the block to the blockchain and is rewarded with newly created Bitcoins. This reward is the miner's incentive to keep the system running.
- **Security:** The math puzzles are difficult to solve, but easy for the rest of the network to check. This process, known as **Proof-of-Work (PoW),** is secure

because it would take an enormous amount of computing power to trick the system.

Mining is what keeps Bitcoin's blockchain secure and decentralized. However, the process requires a lot of electricity, which has raised concerns about its environmental impact.

MINTING: A GREENER ALTERNATIVE

Not all cryptocurrencies are mined in this energy-intensive way. Many newer cryptocurrencies use a different process called **minting**, which is part of a system known as **Proof-of-Stake (PoS)**.

Here's how it works:

- **Staking:** Instead of miners racing to solve puzzles, people who own some of the cryptocurrency (known as "stakers") put a portion of their coins up as collateral. They essentially "stake" their coins to participate in validating new transactions and adding blocks to the blockchain.

- **Selection:** The network randomly selects one of these stakers to validate the next block. The more cryptocurrency someone stakes, the higher their chances of being chosen to validate a block and earn rewards.

- **Eco-Friendly:** Since Proof-of-Stake doesn't require massive amounts of computing power, it's seen as a much more environmentally friendly alternative to mining. Ethereum, for example, has transitioned from Proof-of-Work to Proof-of-Stake to reduce its environmental impact.

THE HALVING: BITCOIN'S SCARCITY TRICK

One of the things that makes Bitcoin so special is its limited supply. There will only ever be 21 million Bitcoins, and this limit is hardcoded into its system.

To control the rate at which new Bitcoins are created, there's a process called the **halving**. Every four years or so, the reward that miners receive for adding a new block is cut in half. This makes Bitcoin scarcer over time, which is why it's often compared to gold—there's only so much of it, and once it's all mined, no more can be created.

IS MINING PROFITABLE?

Many people wonder if mining is a good way to make money. In the early days of Bitcoin, mining was pretty profitable for anyone with a decent computer. But as more people joined the network and the puzzles got harder, mining became more competitive. Today, to be a successful Bitcoin miner, you need specialized hardware and access to cheap electricity.

For other cryptocurrencies that use Proof-of-Stake, you can earn rewards just by holding and staking your coins, which is a lot easier than setting up a mining rig. However, the amount you can earn from staking depends on how much cryptocurrency you own and how the network is designed.

IS ONE BETTER THAN THE OTHER?

Proof-of-Work (mining) and Proof-of-Stake (minting) both have their strengths and weaknesses. Mining is incredibly secure but energy-intensive, while staking is more eco-friendly but relies on users already owning a significant amount of cryptocurrency to participate. Both methods are essential for keeping their respective networks running smoothly.

Chapter 9: How to Actually Buy, Trade, and Use Cryptocurrency

Alright, now that you've got a handle on how cryptocurrencies are made, you might be wondering how to actually get your hands on some! Don't worry—buying, trading, and using cryptocurrencies isn't as complicated as it sounds. In this chapter, we'll walk you through the basics of entering the world of crypto.

STEP 1: CHOOSING A CRYPTO WALLET

Before you can buy any cryptocurrency, you'll need a **crypto wallet**. But don't worry, this isn't a physical wallet like the one you keep in your pocket. A crypto wallet is a digital tool that stores your cryptocurrency and allows you to send and receive it.

There are two main types of wallets:

- **Hot Wallets:** These are connected to the internet, making them convenient for everyday use. You can access them from your phone or computer, but because they're online, they're more vulnerable to hacking. Examples include mobile apps like Coinbase Wallet or Trust Wallet.
- **Cold Wallets:** These are offline wallets, usually in the form of a physical device (like a USB stick) or even a piece of paper with a printed key. They're much more secure but less convenient for frequent transactions. Examples include hardware wallets like Ledger or Trezor.

STEP 2: BUYING CRYPTOCURRENCY

Once you have a wallet, the next step is to buy some cryptocurrency. The easiest way to do this is through a **crypto exchange**—a platform where you can buy, sell, and trade various cryptocurrencies.

Popular exchanges include:

- **Coinbase:** A beginner-friendly platform that's great for new users.
- **Binance:** Offers a wide range of cryptocurrencies and lower fees, but can be a bit more complex.
- **Kraken:** Known for security and offering a variety of digital assets.

On these platforms, you can buy cryptocurrency with regular money (like dollars or euros). You'll need to connect your bank account or use a credit card to make the purchase. Once you've bought some cryptocurrency, it will show up in your exchange account, and you can transfer it to your personal wallet for safekeeping.

STEP 3: TRADING CRYPTOCURRENCY

Now that you've got some crypto, you can either hold onto it (also called **HODLing**) in the hopes that its value increases over time, or you can trade it for other cryptocurrencies. Many exchanges allow you to swap one type of cryptocurrency for another, like converting Bitcoin into Ethereum or Litecoin.

- **Market Orders vs. Limit Orders:** When trading, you'll have the option to place different types of orders. A **market order** buys or sells at the current price, while a **limit order** lets you set a specific price you're willing to buy or sell at. The trade only happens if the market reaches your limit price.

- **Volatility:** Be aware that cryptocurrency prices can change very quickly. What's worth $100 today could be worth $80 tomorrow—or $120! It's this volatility that makes crypto exciting but also risky.

STEP 4: USING CRYPTOCURRENCY

Cryptocurrencies aren't just for holding or trading—you can actually use them for a variety of purposes. More and more businesses are accepting cryptocurrencies as payment, and the list keeps growing. You can use Bitcoin to buy things like electronics, plane tickets, or even a cup of coffee at certain shops.

- **Payment Processors:** Some companies, like **BitPay** or **CoinGate**, help businesses accept cryptocurrency without worrying about the technical details. These processors convert your crypto into regular

money for the merchant, making it easier for everyone.
- **Direct Transfers:** You can also send cryptocurrency directly to someone else, anywhere in the world, without needing a bank or middleman. All you need is the recipient's wallet address, and the transaction can be completed in minutes—often with lower fees than traditional bank transfers.

STEP 5: KEEPING YOUR CRYPTO SAFE

Cryptocurrency transactions are irreversible, so it's crucial to keep your digital assets secure. Here are a few basic security tips:

- **Enable Two-Factor Authentication (2FA):** Always use 2FA on your exchange and wallet accounts to add an extra layer of protection.

- **Use Cold Storage for Large Holdings:** If you have a significant amount of crypto, consider moving it to a cold wallet to protect it from hackers.
- **Double-Check Wallet Addresses:** When sending crypto, double-check the recipient's wallet address. A small mistake can send your funds to the wrong place, and there's no way to reverse it.

WHAT ABOUT TAXES?

In most countries, cryptocurrency is treated as an asset, like stocks or real estate, which means you might owe taxes when you sell it at a profit. Be sure to check your local laws and keep good records of your trades and transactions. Many exchanges offer tools to help track your transactions for tax purposes.

Cryptocurrency might seem intimidating at first, but once you understand the basics of wallets, exchanges, and security, it becomes much easier to manage. Whether you're holding for the long term, actively trading, or just using it to buy a pizza, entering the crypto world can be a smooth and exciting journey.

Chapter 10: The Good, The Bad, and The Ugly of Cryptocurrencies

Cryptocurrencies can seem like a magical solution to many of the problems with traditional finance, but they're not without their challenges. In this chapter, we'll explore the upsides, the downsides, and the potential pitfalls of cryptocurrencies.

THE GOOD: FREEDOM, ACCESSIBILITY, AND INNOVATION

Let's start with why so many people are excited about cryptocurrencies.

- **Financial Freedom:** Cryptocurrencies allow anyone to participate in the financial system without needing a bank account or credit card. This is especially valuable in countries where access to traditional banking is limited. All you need is a smartphone and an internet connection, and you're in.

- **Borderless Transactions:** Cryptocurrencies make it easy to send money across borders without the delays and fees of traditional banking systems. You can send Bitcoin to someone halfway across the world in minutes, with little to no extra cost.
- **Decentralization:** Because cryptocurrencies aren't controlled by any government or corporation, they offer a level of independence and freedom from centralized control. This is particularly appealing to people who don't trust their local banking systems or governments.
- **Innovation:** Cryptocurrencies are paving the way for all kinds of new technologies and industries. From decentralized finance

(DeFi) to digital art (NFTs), they're driving innovation in ways that were hard to imagine a decade ago. Blockchain technology itself offers endless possibilities beyond money.

THE BAD: RISKS, SCAMS, AND VOLATILITY

Of course, it's not all sunshine and rainbows. Cryptocurrencies come with significant risks that everyone should be aware of.

- **Price Volatility:** Cryptocurrencies are notorious for their wild price swings. One day your Bitcoin might be worth $60,000, and the next it could drop to $40,000. This makes cryptocurrencies exciting but also risky as an investment. Some people have made fortunes, while others have lost huge amounts of money overnight.

- **Security Risks:** While blockchain technology itself is very secure, that doesn't mean your crypto is always safe. Hacks and scams are a constant threat in the crypto world. If your exchange or wallet gets hacked, your funds could disappear forever. And remember: there are no refunds in crypto!
- **Lack of Regulation:** Cryptocurrencies operate in a legal gray area in many countries. While this gives users more freedom, it also means there's less protection if something goes wrong. If an exchange goes bankrupt or runs off with your money, there might be little you can do about it.
- **Environmental Concerns:** Proof-of-Work cryptocurrencies like Bitcoin require massive amounts of energy to mine. This has led to criticism over their environmental impact, especially as the world grapples with climate change. Some newer cryptocurrencies use more

eco-friendly alternatives like Proof-of-Stake, but the debate over energy use is ongoing.

THE UGLY: SCAMS AND ILLEGAL ACTIVITIES

Finally, let's talk about the not-so-pretty side of cryptocurrencies. Unfortunately, the relative anonymity and lack of regulation in the crypto world have made it a target for scammers and criminals.

- **Scams and Ponzi Schemes:** Crypto is full of get-rich-quick schemes and shady investment opportunities. From fake coins to fraudulent exchanges, there are countless ways to get scammed if you're not careful. Always do your research before investing in any cryptocurrency.
- **Ransomware and Dark Web Use:** Because cryptocurrency transactions can

be anonymous, they've become popular for illegal activities like ransomware attacks and buying illegal goods on the dark web. While this isn't the fault of cryptocurrencies themselves, it has given them a somewhat shady reputation in some circles.

- **Regulatory Crackdowns:** Governments around the world are still figuring out how to regulate cryptocurrencies. In some places, authorities have cracked down hard on crypto trading and mining, making it difficult or even illegal to participate. The uncertainty around future regulations can add another layer of risk for users and investors.

BALANCING THE GOOD WITH THE RISKS

Despite the risks, many people believe the benefits of cryptocurrencies outweigh the downsides. Cryptos represent a new way of thinking about money, ownership, and trust. But it's important to enter this space with your eyes open, knowing both the rewards and the dangers.

Cryptocurrencies have the potential to reshape industries, empower people who don't have access to traditional banking, and offer new ways to interact with technology. But they also come with real risks, from price volatility to scams. Whether you're investing or just curious, understanding both sides of the coin is key to navigating this new digital landscape.

Chapter 11: Blockchains in the Real World (More Than Just Money)

By now, you probably associate blockchains with cryptocurrencies like Bitcoin and Ethereum. But here's something you might not know—blockchains have so much more to offer beyond digital money. From healthcare to supply chains, blockchains are already being used in ways that can transform how industries work. Let's take a look at some real-world applications.

SUPPLY CHAIN MANAGEMENT: TRACKING GOODS FROM START TO FINISH

One of the most exciting uses of blockchain technology is in **supply chain management**. Imagine you're buying a bar of chocolate and you want to know if it was ethically sourced. With blockchain, you could track every step of that chocolate's journey—from the cocoa farm to the factory, and from the warehouse to your local store.

Here's how it works:

- Each time the product moves through the supply chain, a new "block" of data is added to the blockchain. This might include who handled the product, where it's been, and even the conditions during shipping (like temperature).
- Since the blockchain is transparent and secure, everyone from producers to

consumers can verify that the information is accurate and hasn't been tampered with.

Major companies, like Walmart and IBM, are already using blockchain technology to improve transparency in their supply chains. This can help prevent fraud, ensure product quality, and even reduce the risk of counterfeiting.

VOTING: MAKING ELECTIONS MORE SECURE

In many parts of the world, voting is vulnerable to fraud and manipulation. Blockchain could solve this by creating a **tamper-proof voting system**.

- Every vote could be recorded as a block on the blockchain, ensuring it can't be altered once it's cast.

- Voters could verify that their vote was counted, but the system would still protect their privacy.
- Because the blockchain is decentralized, no single party could control or manipulate the results.

Blockchain-based voting systems are still in the experimental phase, but they offer the potential for more secure, transparent, and trustworthy elections.

HEALTHCARE: SECURING PATIENT DATA

Another promising use for blockchain technology is in **healthcare**. Managing patient records is tricky because they need to be easily accessible by doctors but also highly secure to protect patient privacy. Blockchain can offer both.

- Medical records could be stored on a blockchain, ensuring they are secure and only accessible to authorized healthcare providers.
- Patients could control who has access to their data, and healthcare providers could share records more easily, reducing the need for repeated tests or procedures.
- Blockchain could also help with drug traceability, ensuring that medications are genuine and haven't been tampered with during production or delivery.

Several companies are already working on blockchain-based healthcare solutions, and the technology could help reduce medical errors, improve efficiency, and keep patient data safe.

NFTS: REVOLUTIONIZING ART, MUSIC, AND COLLECTIBLES

You've probably heard of **NFTs** (non-fungible tokens)—digital assets that represent ownership of a unique item, often art or music. NFTs have exploded in popularity because they allow creators to sell their work directly to buyers without needing an intermediary like a gallery or record label.

- An NFT is a unique token stored on a blockchain, which proves ownership of a digital asset (like a piece of art, a song, or even a tweet).
- Artists can sell their work as NFTs and even program royalties into the token, so they get paid every time the NFT is resold.
- NFTs are already being used for digital collectibles, virtual real estate, and even tickets to exclusive events.

While some see NFTs as a passing trend, others believe they represent a new way for creators to monetize their work in the digital age.

FIGHTING CLIMATE CHANGE: BLOCKCHAIN FOR CARBON TRACKING

Believe it or not, blockchain technology can also be used to combat **climate change**. By creating transparent, verifiable records of carbon emissions, blockchain can help companies and governments track their environmental impact and take steps to reduce it.

- Blockchain can be used to verify carbon credits, ensuring that companies meet their climate goals by reducing their carbon footprint.
- Projects like **Energy Web** are using blockchain to help track renewable energy

production and create more efficient energy grids.

Blockchain's transparency and security make it an ideal tool for ensuring that environmental data is accurate and trustworthy, helping us hold companies and governments accountable for their impact on the planet.

OTHER APPLICATIONS: WHAT ELSE CAN BLOCKCHAINS DO?

- **Real Estate:** Blockchain can simplify the process of buying and selling property by recording property transactions on a public ledger. This reduces paperwork and speeds up the process.
- **Identity Management:** Governments and companies are exploring blockchain to securely store identity documents, reducing the risk of identity theft and fraud.

- **Intellectual Property:** Blockchain can be used to protect intellectual property rights by proving who created a piece of content first and who owns it.

Blockchains are proving to be far more than just a way to track digital money. Whether it's improving transparency in supply chains, revolutionizing healthcare, or even fighting climate change, blockchain technology is already making a real-world impact. As industries continue to explore and adopt this technology, we can expect to see even more innovative uses in the future.

Chapter 12: Can Blockchain Really Change the World?

Now that we've explored all the different ways blockchain technology can be used—from cryptocurrencies to healthcare to voting—it's time to ask the big question: Can blockchain actually change the world? In this final chapter, we'll take a look at the potential future of blockchain and the impact it could have on society.

DECENTRALIZATION: A WORLD WITHOUT MIDDLEMEN?

One of the core ideas behind blockchain is **decentralization**. Imagine a world where we don't need banks, governments, or corporations to manage important services.

Instead, we rely on decentralized networks where trust is built into the system, thanks to blockchain technology.

- **Banking the Unbanked:** In many parts of the world, people don't have access to traditional banking services. Blockchain could provide a solution by enabling secure financial transactions for anyone with a smartphone. With cryptocurrencies, people could send money, take out loans, and participate in global trade, all without needing a bank.
- **Freedom from Censorship:** Decentralized platforms could help prevent censorship, as no single authority would be able to control or shut down a blockchain. This has powerful implications for free speech and access to information in countries with restrictive governments.
- **Ownership of Personal Data:** In a blockchain-powered world, individuals could have complete control over their

personal data. Instead of companies like Facebook or Google owning your information, you could choose who gets access to your data and how it's used. This could revolutionize privacy and how we interact with online services.

SMART CONTRACTS AND DAPPS: TRANSFORMING INDUSTRIES

As we discussed earlier, smart contracts and decentralized apps (dApps) have the potential to automate and streamline a wide range of industries. But how far can this technology go?

- **Automated Business Models:** Imagine a company that runs entirely on smart contracts. Everything from payroll to customer service could be automated, reducing costs and increasing efficiency. Decentralized Autonomous Organizations (DAOs) are already experimenting with this idea, allowing groups to make decisions and manage resources without a traditional management structure.

- **The Gig Economy 2.0:** Platforms like Uber or Airbnb could be replaced by decentralized versions, where the platform itself is run by the users. With smart contracts, drivers and riders could connect directly, splitting the earnings fairly without a middleman taking a cut.

CHALLENGES TO MASS ADOPTION

Of course, there are still significant challenges before blockchain can fully realize its potential.

- **Scalability:** Right now, many blockchain networks struggle with scalability. Bitcoin and Ethereum, for example, can handle only a limited number of transactions per second, which makes it difficult for them to compete with traditional systems like Visa or Mastercard. However, solutions like Layer 2 scaling and new consensus mechanisms are being developed to address this.

- **Energy Consumption:** The environmental impact of Proof-of-Work blockchains like Bitcoin is a hot topic. While Proof-of-Stake systems are more eco-friendly, finding a balance between security and sustainability will be critical for blockchain's future.

- **Regulation:** Governments around the world are still figuring out how to regulate cryptocurrencies and blockchain technology. Too much regulation could stifle innovation, but too little could lead to issues like fraud and market instability. Striking the right balance will be key to blockchain's widespread acceptance.

COULD BLOCKCHAINS REPLACE GOVERNMENTS?

Some enthusiasts imagine a future where blockchain replaces not just banks and corporations, but even governments.

- **Voting and Governance:** As we've seen with blockchain-based voting systems, this technology could make elections more secure and transparent. Blockchain could also be used for **digital identity systems**, ensuring that everyone has a secure and verifiable identity without relying on central authorities.

- **Taxation and Public Services:** With smart contracts, taxes could be collected automatically based on real-time economic data, and public funds could be allocated more efficiently. Imagine a system where citizens can track every dollar spent by the government on public services, ensuring complete transparency.

THE BIGGER PICTURE: A MORE TRUSTED, CONNECTED WORLD

At its heart, blockchain is about **trust**. By creating systems that are transparent, secure, and decentralized, blockchain could change how we interact with everything from money to social media to government services.

- **Global Collaboration:** Blockchain could make it easier for people and organizations across the globe to collaborate without needing to trust each other directly. Whether it's sharing data, forming partnerships, or building businesses, blockchain provides a foundation of trust that could bring people closer together.
- **Empowerment:** Perhaps the most exciting potential of blockchain is its ability to empower individuals. By giving people control over their own data, assets, and identities, blockchain could level the playing field in a way that's never been done before.

A FUTURE FULL OF POSSIBILITIES

The future of blockchain is full of possibilities, but it's important to remember that we're still in the early days. Blockchain technology is still evolving, and we don't yet know all the ways it will impact the world. What we do know is that it has the potential to revolutionize industries, empower individuals, and build a more connected, transparent, and trusted world.

Blockchain might not change everything overnight, but its potential to reshape the way we interact with technology, money, and even each other is undeniable. Whether it's in finance, governance, or simply making the internet a more secure and fair place, blockchain is already starting to leave its mark on the world—and the journey is just beginning.

Conclusion: What You've Learned and What's Next

By now, you've learned what a blockchain is, how cryptocurrencies like Bitcoin work, and how this technology is being used beyond just money. You've seen both the risks and rewards of diving into the world of crypto and blockchain, and you have a sense of where the future might take us.

If you're curious to explore more, the next step could be trying out some of the technologies we've talked about. Maybe buy a small amount of cryptocurrency, experiment with a decentralized app, or just follow the latest developments in this exciting space. Whatever you do, know that you're now part of the conversation about the future of technology and trust.

Glossary of Key Terms

Altcoin:

Any cryptocurrency that is not Bitcoin. Examples include Ethereum, Litecoin, and Ripple. These coins often have different features from Bitcoin, like faster transactions or different consensus mechanisms.

Blockchain:

A decentralized digital ledger that records transactions in a secure, transparent, and tamper-proof way. Blocks of data are linked together in a chain, and once added, they cannot be altered.

Block:

A collection of transaction data that is recorded on a blockchain. Each block contains a unique code (hash) and the hash of the previous block, which links it to the chain.

Consensus Mechanism:
The method used by a blockchain network to agree on the validity of transactions. Two common consensus mechanisms are Proof-of-Work (PoW) and Proof-of-Stake (PoS).

Cryptocurrency:
A type of digital or virtual currency that uses cryptography for security. Cryptocurrencies are decentralized and often run on blockchain technology. Bitcoin and Ethereum are examples of cryptocurrencies.

Decentralization:
A system where control is distributed across many nodes (computers) rather than being concentrated in a single authority like a bank or government. In a decentralized network, no single party controls the data or decisions.

dApp (Decentralized Application):
An application that runs on a blockchain network rather than a centralized server.

dApps are powered by smart contracts and operate independently once they are deployed.

Digital Wallet (Crypto Wallet):
A tool that allows users to store, send, and receive cryptocurrency. Digital wallets can be "hot" (connected to the internet) or "cold" (offline for greater security).

Ethereum:
A blockchain platform that allows developers to build decentralized apps (dApps) and create smart contracts. Its cryptocurrency is called Ether (ETH). Ethereum is famous for its flexibility and use of smart contracts.

Hash:
A unique string of characters (like a digital fingerprint) generated by a cryptographic function. Each block in a blockchain has a hash, and even a small change in the block's data will produce a completely different hash.

HODL:
A slang term in the crypto community meaning to hold onto cryptocurrency rather than selling it, especially during periods of market volatility. The term originated from a misspelled online post.

Immutable:
A feature of blockchains that means once data is recorded in a block, it cannot be altered or deleted. This makes blockchain data trustworthy and secure.

Mining:
The process of using computing power to solve complex mathematical problems in order to validate transactions and add new blocks to the blockchain. In return, miners are rewarded with new cryptocurrency. This process is central to Proof-of-Work blockchains like Bitcoin.

NFT (Non-Fungible Token):

A type of digital asset that represents ownership of a unique item, such as art, music, or collectibles. NFTs are stored on a blockchain and cannot be replicated or exchanged on a one-to-one basis like cryptocurrencies.

Node:

A computer that participates in the blockchain network by keeping a copy of the blockchain and helping to validate transactions. Nodes communicate with each other to reach consensus on the state of the blockchain.

Peer-to-Peer (P2P):

A system where transactions or exchanges happen directly between users without needing a central authority or intermediary. Blockchain transactions are often peer-to-peer.

Proof-of-Work (PoW):

A consensus mechanism where miners compete to solve complex mathematical puzzles in order to validate transactions and add new blocks to the blockchain. Bitcoin uses Proof-of-Work.

Proof-of-Stake (PoS):
A more energy-efficient consensus mechanism where participants (stakers) lock up some of their cryptocurrency as collateral, and the network randomly selects one to validate the next block. Ethereum has transitioned to Proof-of-Stake.

Private Key:
A secret string of letters and numbers that allows you to access and control your cryptocurrency in your wallet. It's like a password, and if you lose it, you lose access to your funds.

Public Key:
A cryptographic code that is used to receive cryptocurrency. It's like your bank account number—anyone can send funds to it, but only you can access the funds using your private key.

Smart Contract:

A self-executing contract with the terms of the agreement directly written into code. Smart contracts automatically enforce agreements and are often used in decentralized applications (dApps).

Staking:

The process of participating in a Proof-of-Stake (PoS) blockchain by locking up a certain amount of cryptocurrency in the network. Stakers help validate transactions and can earn rewards for doing so.

Token:

A unit of value issued on a blockchain. Tokens can represent anything from currency (like Bitcoin or Ether) to assets, votes, or even digital collectibles (like NFTs).

Transaction Fee:

A small fee paid to the network to process a transaction. The fee incentivizes miners or validators to include the transaction in the next block.

Trustless System:

A system where participants don't need to know or trust each other to transact safely. Blockchain achieves this through its decentralized nature and cryptographic security.

Volatility:

The rapid and significant price swings often seen in cryptocurrencies. Due to high volatility, the value of cryptocurrencies like Bitcoin can fluctuate wildly over short periods of time.

www.ingramcontent.com/pod-product-compliance
Lightning Source LLC
Chambersburg PA
CBHW070154230526
45471CB00002B/654